English Grammar

LEARN IN AN HOUR

RAMADAS ABBOY

PREFACE

Grammar teaches the right way to speak and write.

In grammar textbooks, a lot of times, the emphasis is placed on the description of the parts of the sentences and its structure. For some, it can be hard and intimidating to learn grammar this way. This book is written for others, focusing more on language than on grammar. I have underlined the "grammar" in the sentences. Read this book like a storybook. Reading this multiple times gives a firmer grasp on the grammatical language.

This is not a comprehensive grammar textbook.

I would like to thank Sridevi, Samyuktha Krishna, and Elisa Quion for their help in making this book possible. My thanks are also due to my grandchildren Anika, Brijesh, Krishna, Vishnu, and Arjun for their input and ideas.

RAMADAS ABBOY

Maria is a girl.

Jack saved money to buy a book.

Lakshmi lives in India.

Bobby made a nice meal.

Khan is a good boy.

Tokyo is a big city.

Berlin is the capital of Germany.

You made a good decision.

I must have courage.

I want to visit <u>Japan</u>.

<u>Chinese</u> food tastes very good.

<u>New Delhi</u> is the capital of <u>India</u>.

<u>Mexican</u> people speak <u>Spanish.</u>

<u>Singapore</u> is a beautiful <u>city</u>.

I love to eat <u>candies</u>.

There are too many <u>mangoes</u> in this tree.

There are many <u>churches</u> on this road.

Some Plurals are different.

child	**children**
woman	**women**
man	**men**
bus	**buses**
glass	**glasses**
person	**people**
potato	**potatoes**
knife	**knives**
city	**cities**
foot	**feet**
tooth	**teeth**
lady	**ladies**
baby	**babies**
leaf	**leaves**

This book belongs to Krishna.

This is <u>Krishna's</u> book.

Leela is the sister of Meena.

<u>Leela's</u> sister is Meena.

<u>Meena's</u> sister is Leela.

Lilly said that <u>Lilly</u> is going to see <u>Lilly's</u> sister. (wrong)

Lilly said that <u>she</u> is going to see <u>her</u> sister.

<u>Park</u> is a student.

<u>He</u> is a student.

<u>Beverly</u> is a good girl.

<u>She</u> is a good girl.

<u>He</u> is tall.

<u>She</u> is my friend.

<u>It</u> is a notebook.

I am good.

You are good.

He is good.

She is good.

We are good.

They are good.

It is good.

It is <u>mine</u>.

That is <u>yours</u>.

It is <u>his</u> book.

It is <u>her</u> book.

It is <u>our</u> book.

It is <u>your</u> book.

It is <u>their</u> book.

How many did you buy?

How often do you buy?

How did you buy?

Which did you buy?

Where did you buy?

When did you buy?

What did you buy?

Why did you buy?

Who helped you to buy?

<u>Who</u> wants to go to the bazaar today?

You may go to school with <u>whomever</u> you like.

You may choose <u>whichever</u> dress you want to wear.

You can go <u>wherever</u> you want to go.

Give it to <u>whomever</u> asks.

I went to a movie by <u>myself</u>.

The baby sat up by <u>himself</u>.

The baby sat up by <u>herself</u>.

The fruit fell from the tree by <u>itself</u>.

We cooked the food by <u>ourselves</u>.

<u>This</u> is mine.

<u>That</u> tree is tall.

<u>These</u> are good bananas.

<u>Those</u> are rotten bananas.

Someone gave me money to buy books.

Everyone is going to town.

Anyone can do it.

Something is not good.

Nothing went wrong.

Everything is very good.

Somebody can do it.

Anybody can do it.

Everybody is good.

Nobody can do it.

A <u>few</u> people went to the party.

<u>Some</u> people went to the party.

<u>Many</u> people went to the party.

<u>Several</u> people went to the party.

<u>Each</u> person brought his own book.

<u>All</u> of the boys ate their food.

<u>Only</u> one student failed the exam.

<u>Most</u> of us like to watch TV.

Master list of some Pronouns

all	itself	that
another	many	they
anybody	me	their
anyone	mine	theirs
anything	my	them
both	myself	themselves
each	neither	these
either	nobody	this
everybody	none	those
everyone	no one	us
everything	nothing	we

Master list of some Pronouns

few	others	what
he	our	which
him	ours	who
himself	ourselves	whom
his	several	whose
her	she	you
hers	some	your
herself	somebody	yours
I	someone	yourself
It	something	yourselves

That is an idea. That is a <u>great</u> idea.

There are trees. There are <u>three</u> trees.

People came late. <u>Several</u> people came late.

I have a dress. I have a <u>pink</u> dress.

The <u>hungry</u> baby was crying.

The player was <u>tired</u> and <u>hungry</u>.

The new bicycles are <u>expensive</u>.

Brijesh arrived <u>early</u>.

Kim will come <u>late</u> in the evening.

Hashimoto lives in a <u>nice big</u> house.

The floor had been damaged by <u>heavy</u> rain.

The trees were destroyed in a <u>big</u> storm.

The parcel was sent by <u>express</u> train.

Give me <u>a</u> book.

Give me <u>the</u> book.

Give me <u>an</u> apple.

Give me <u>the</u> apple.

I left <u>the</u> bag at home.

Can you close <u>the</u> door, please?

<u>The</u> Taj Mahal is beautiful.

He played <u>the</u> flute.

a   an   the

Manila is the capital of the Philippines.

Krishna is a student.

Brazil is a very big country.

Everyone wants to be happy.

Arjun had to make a decision.

You must be good.

Several people went to the party.

Many people went to the party.

Some people went to the party.

Only one girl went to the party.

Most of us went to the party.

I am <u>strong</u>.

I am <u>stronger</u> than you.

I am the <u>strongest</u>.

good	better	best
strong	stronger	strongest
big	bigger	biggest
careful	more careful	most careful
successful	more successful	most successful
generous	less generous	least generous
generous	more generous	most generous
funny	funnier	funniest

I <u>am</u> good.

He <u>is</u> good.

She <u>is</u> good.

You <u>are</u> good.

We <u>are</u> good.

They <u>are</u> good.

It <u>is</u> good.

I sing.

I sang.

I am singing.

I was singing.

I have been singing.

I had been singing.

I will sing.

I will be singing.

I would have been singing.

I can sing.

I could sing.

<u>Can</u> I sing?

<u>Could</u> I sing?

<u>Shall</u> I sing?

<u>Should</u> I sing?

<u>Is</u> it okay to sing?

He <u>works</u>.

He <u>worked</u>.

He <u>is working</u>.

He <u>was working</u>.

He <u>will work</u>.

He <u>will be working</u>.

He <u>has been working</u>.

He <u>had been working</u>.

<u>Have</u> you <u>been working</u>?

I <u>have been working</u>.

I <u>see</u> him.

I <u>saw</u> him.

I <u>will see</u> him.

I <u>will be seeing</u> him.

I <u>would</u> like to see him.

I <u>want</u> to see him.

I <u>have</u> to see him.

I <u>must</u> see him.

I <u>should</u> see him.

I <u>can</u> see him.

I <u>could</u> see him.

I <u>have seen</u> him.

I <u>have not seen</u> him.

Some Irregular Verbs

Infinitive	Past Simple	Past Participle
cost	cost	cost
cut	cut	cut
hit	hit	hit
let	let	let
put	put	put
set	set	set
split	split	split
begin	began	begun
bite	bit	bitten
drink	drank	drunk

Some Irregular Verbs

Infinitive	Past Simple	Past Participle
drive	drove	driven
fall	fell	fallen
forget	forgot	forgotten
eat	ate	eaten
freeze	froze	frozen
speak	spoke	spoken
sing	sang	sung
take	took	taken
know	knew	known
write	wrote	written

I <u>can</u> get it.

I <u>could</u> get it.

I <u>may</u> get it.

I <u>might</u> get it.

I <u>will</u> get it.

I <u>will have</u> to get it.

I <u>would</u> get it.

I <u>shall</u> get it.

I <u>should</u> get it.

I <u>have</u> to get it.

I <u>must</u> get it.

I <u>ought</u> to get it.

You should read.

You should read a lot.

You should read now.

You should read here.

You should read fast.

You should read faster.

You should read well.

I should read.

I should read a lot.

I should read now.

I should read here.

I should read fast.

I should read faster.

I should read well.

<u>Shall</u> I turn on the light?

<u>Should</u> I turn on the light?

<u>Could</u> I turn on the light?

It <u>will</u> be possible.

It <u>will</u> not be possible.

It <u>should</u> be possible.

May I leave early <u>if</u> I finish my job?

<u>Unless</u> you finish your job, you cannot leave.

<u>Do</u> you <u>like</u> apples?

<u>Did</u> you <u>finish</u> your job?

Have you <u>done</u> your job?

Vishnu <u>does</u> his job <u>well</u>.

Are you <u>doing</u> your job?

I <u>am doing</u> my job.

do   does   did   done   doing

It's raining.

It's getting late.

It's about two miles.

It's hot.

It's time to go.

It's not too far.

I <u>don't</u> like it.

do not   <u>don't</u>

did not   <u>didn't</u>

cannot   <u>can't</u>

could not   <u>couldn't</u>

should not   <u>shouldn't</u>

would not   <u>wouldn't</u>

has not   <u>hasn't</u>

have not   <u>haven't</u>

had not   <u>hadn't</u>

You walk <u>slowly</u>.

You run <u>quickly</u>.

You speak <u>softly</u>.

Close the door <u>gently</u>.

She is <u>nice</u>.

You are <u>late</u>.

I felt <u>happy</u>.

It <u>smells</u> good.

It <u>looks</u> good.

It <u>seems</u> good.

It <u>is</u> good.

It <u>tastes</u> good.

It <u>remains</u> good.

It <u>appears</u> good.

It <u>feels</u> good.

Sheila <u>and</u> Leela went to school together.

He is smart <u>and</u> hard working.

Chan missed school <u>because</u> he was sick.

I will not surrender <u>until</u> I win.

He is smart <u>but</u> lazy.

I want to study well <u>so that</u> I can get a good job.

<u>After</u> the movie was over we all went home.

<u>Neither</u> my brother <u>nor</u> me can come tonight.

<u>Either</u> my brother <u>or</u> I will come tonight.

I <u>don't</u> know what happened!

<u>Hello</u>, how are you?

<u>Sorry</u>, I don't know the answer.

I <u>won</u>!

That <u>hurts</u>.

Isn't that <u>pretty</u>?

WHERE?

<u>at</u> home

<u>before</u> that building

<u>by</u> the shop

<u>from</u> here to there

<u>in</u> the school

<u>on</u> the table

<u>under</u> the table

<u>behind</u> the table

in <u>front</u> of the table

<u>next</u> to the table

<u>besides</u> the table

<u>opposite</u> to that table

<u>in between</u> the tables

<u>in the middle</u> of the ground

<u>near</u> the table

<u>not far from</u> the table

WHEN?

I will be home <u>by</u> 5 PM.

<u>at</u> 9 a.m.

<u>before</u> 9 a.m.

<u>until</u> 9 a.m.

<u>since</u> 9 a.m.

<u>about</u> 9 a.m.

<u>after</u> 9 a.m.

<u>by</u> 9 a.m.

<u>from</u> 9 a.m.

It's <u>exactly</u> three o'clock.

It's <u>just</u> about three o'clock.

It's <u>about</u> three o'clock.

It's <u>nearly</u> three o'clock.

It's <u>almost</u> three o'clock.

<u>It's</u> three o'clock.

It is a lovely day, <u>isn't it</u>?

You know Anika, <u>don't you</u>?

They played well, <u>didn't they</u>?

PUNCTUATION

I am done.

Unless you read well, you cannot pass.

There was a book, pen and pencil in the bag.

What are you doing?

He said, "don't come late".

It was raining; the traffic slowed down.

I am very happy!

The Bible says: Love thy neighbor as thy self

unmarried

non-smoker

ex-president

darkness

homeless

careless

careful

Hello.

May I help you?

Can you help me?

Thank you.

I'm sorry.

Excuse me.

Excuse me, please.

After you

May I come in?

Could you spell it, please?

May I borrow your pen?

I am wrong.

Help yourself.

Happy birthday.

Congratulations!

Hope to see you soon.

Have a nice day.

Drive safely.

Are you okay?

What can I do for you?

Maybe later.

Push.

Pull.

Insert the coins in the slot.

I want.

I want to go to school.

I want to go to a school.

I want to go to this school.

I want to go to this school because it is the best school.

I asked.

I asked Chris.

I asked Chris for a job.

I asked Chris for a job, but he said that he was not hiring.

I feel happy today.

I feel extremely happy today.

I feel extremely happy today because it's my birthday.

I feel extremely happy today because it's my birthday and all my friends came to my party.

The tall boy in the front yard is my brother.

My brother is the tall boy in the front yard.

The boy who is tall in the front yard is my brother.

GRAMMAR

Simplified meaning

---

1. Noun: Name, person, place, thing,
               amount, qualities

               Eg: <u>Lee</u>, <u>cat</u>, <u>ball</u>, <u>courage</u>

2. Pronoun: Replaces noun.

               Eg: <u>he</u>, <u>it</u>

3. Adjectives: Description of a noun or
               pronoun

               Eg: <u>beautiful</u> flower

4. Verb: Action. Eg: <u>walk</u>

               Tense: present, past or future

               Eg: <u>walked</u>

GRAMMAR

Simplified meaning

5. Adverb:	Describes or modifies the verb.
	Eg: walked <u>faster</u>
6. Prepositions:	Shows relationship between noun/pronoun and another part of sentence.
	Eg: Chen walked <u>to</u> the school
7. Conjunctions:	Words that connect.
	Eg: Krishna <u>and</u> Arjun walked to the school
8. Interjection:	Expresses feelings
	Eg: I am <u>sorry.</u> I am <u>sad.</u>

Eg = example